T0010809

For the
World's
Greatest
M♥m

summersdale

FOR THE WORLD'S GREATEST M♥M

An Hachette UK Company
www.hachette.co.uk

Summersdale Publishers Ltd
Part of Octopus Publishing Group Limited
Carmelite House
50 Victoria Embankment
LONDON
EC4Y 0DZ
UK

www.summersdale.com

Printed and bound in China

ISBN: 978-1-80007-442-2

Substantial discounts on bulk quantities of Summersdale books are available to corporations, professional associations and other organizations. For details contact general enquiries: telephone: +44 (0) 1243 771107 or email: enquiries@summersdale.com.

To ....

From..............................

My mom is
definitely my rock.

ALICIA KEYS

ANY MOTHER
COULD PERFORM
THE JOBS OF
SEVERAL AIR-TRAFFIC
CONTROLLERS
WITH EASE.

LISA ALTHER

There's no doubt that motherhood is the best thing in my life. It's all that really matters.

Courtney Cox

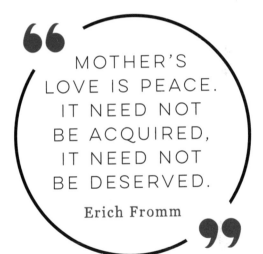

MOTHER'S LOVE IS PEACE. IT NEED NOT BE ACQUIRED, IT NEED NOT BE DESERVED.

Erich Fromm

MY MOTHER
WAS MY ROLE
MODEL BEFORE
I EVEN KNEW
WHAT THAT
WORD WAS.

_____

LISA LESLIE

Family is not an important thing, it's everything.

MICHAEL J. FOX

YOU'RE MY
guiding light

My mother's love
has always been
a sustaining force
for our family.

MICHELLE OBAMA

IT DOESN'T MATTER
HOW **OLD** YOU
ARE, OR WHAT
YOU DO IN YOUR
LIFE, YOU **NEVER**
STOP NEEDING
YOUR MUM.

Kate Winslet

A good mother is worth a hundred teachers.

ITALIAN PROVERB

MOTHERHOOD
MEANT I HAVE
WRITTEN FOUR
FEWER BOOKS,
BUT I KNOW MORE
ABOUT LIFE.

A. S. BYATT

When a child needs a mother to talk to, nobody else but a mother will do.

ERICA JONG

God could not
be everywhere,
and therefore he
made mothers.

RUDYARD KIPLING

The older I get,
the more I see the
power of that young
woman, my mother.

SHARON OLDS

SPENDING
TIME WITH
you
IS MY
FAVOURITE
THING TO
do

I like it when my mother smiles. And I especially like it when I make her smile.

ADRIANA TRIGIANI

A mother is one
to whom you
hurry when you
are troubled.

EMILY DICKINSON

THE FAMILY IS
ONE OF NATURE'S
MASTERPIECES.

GEORGE SANTAYANA

There's no way to be a perfect mother, and a million ways to be a good one.

Jill Churchill

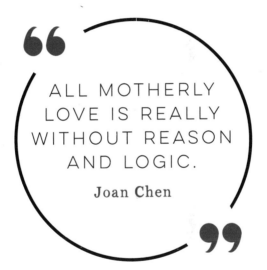

ALL MOTHERLY
LOVE IS REALLY
WITHOUT REASON
AND LOGIC.

Joan Chen

MAMA WAS
MY GREATEST
TEACHER,
A TEACHER OF
COMPASSION,
LOVE AND
FEARLESSNESS.

STEVIE WONDER

If I could do half as good a job as my mom did, I'd be pretty happy.

JENNIFER GARNER

You know

ALL THE WAYS

to make me
feel better

She is pure
unconditional love.
She is grace and mercy.
She is strength and
protection. She is giver
of life. She is a mother.

TARAJI P. HENSON

I GOT TO GROW
UP WITH A
MOTHER WHO
TAUGHT ME TO
BELIEVE IN ME.

Antonio Villaraigosa

Yes, Mother. I can
see you are flawed.
You have not hidden
it. That is your
greatest gift to me.

ALICE WALKER

I WILL ACCEPT LOTS
OF THINGS, BUT NOT
WHEN SOMEONE
INSULTS MY MUM,
THE NICEST PERSON
IN THE WORLD.

ANDY MURRAY

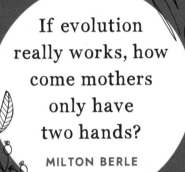

If evolution
really works, how
come mothers
only have
two hands?

MILTON BERLE

When you're sick,
nobody takes
care of you like
your mom.

TRISHA YEARWOOD

A mother's love...
perceives no
impossibilities.

CORNELIA PADDOCK

A mother can do more in half an hour than most people do in a day

SWEATER, NOUN:
A GARMENT WORN
BY A CHILD WHEN
ITS MOTHER IS
FEELING **CHILLY**.

Ambrose Bierce

My mother has
always been my
emotional barometer
and my guidance.

EMMA STONE

FOR WHEN A
CHILD IS BORN THE
MOTHER ALSO IS
BORN AGAIN.

GILBERT PARKER

But behind all your stories is your mother's story, for hers is where yours begins.

Mitch Albom

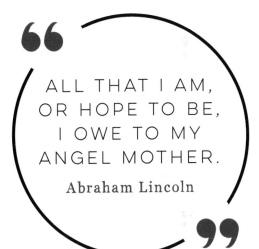

ALL THAT I AM,
OR HOPE TO BE,
I OWE TO MY
ANGEL MOTHER.

Abraham Lincoln

IT TAKES
COURAGE
TO RAISE
CHILDREN.

JOHN STEINBECK

Life began with waking up and loving my mother's face.

GEORGE ELIOT

ALL
MOTHERS
ARE
superheroes

I am sure that
if the mothers of
various nations
could meet,
there would be
no more wars.

E. M. FORSTER

I BELIEVE IN THE **STRENGTH** AND **INTELLIGENCE** AND **SENSITIVITY** OF WOMEN. MY MUM IS A STRONG WOMAN AND I LOVE HER FOR IT.

Tom Hiddleston

Moms are as relentless as the tides. They don't just drive us to practice, they drive us to greatness.

STEVE RUSHIN

WHERE THERE IS
A MOTHER IN THE
HOME, MATTERS
GO WELL.

AMOS BRONSON ALCOTT

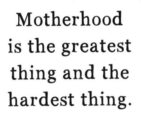

Motherhood
is the greatest
thing and the
hardest thing.

RICKI LAKE

Being a mother is exhausting, but it really is the best job in the world.

SANDRA BULLOCK

My mother is a walking miracle.

LEONARDO DiCAPRIO

I APPRECIATE *everything* YOU DO *for me*

A mother's love for her child is like nothing else in the world.

AGATHA CHRISTIE

I shall never forget my mother, for it was she who planted and nurtured the first seeds of good within me.

IMMANUEL KANT

MY MOTHER IS
EVERYTHING TO ME.
SHE'S MY ANCHOR,
SHE'S THE PERSON
I GO TO WHEN
I NEED TO TALK
TO SOMEONE.

DEMI LOVATO

We all come from women, and there's something extraordinary about the mothers who raised us.

Annie Lennox

A CHILD'S
FIRST TEACHER
IS ITS MOTHER.

Peng Liyuan

THERE IS
NOTHING IN
THE WORLD OF
ART LIKE THE
SONGS MOTHER
USED TO SING.

BILLY SUNDAY

I think in a lot of ways unconditional love is a myth. My mom's the only reason I know it's a real thing.

CONOR OBERST

You always
KNOW JUST
what to say

We have charts,
maps and lists
on the fridge, all
over the house. I
sometimes feel like
I'm with the CIA.

KATE WINSLET

MY MOTHER'S
MENU CONSISTED
OF TWO CHOICES:
TAKE IT OR
LEAVE IT.

Buddy Hackett

A mother is she who can take the place of all others but whose place no one else can take.

GASPARD MERMILLOD

A CHILD IS NOT A
VASE TO BE FILLED,
BUT A FIRE TO BE LIT.

FRANÇOIS RABELAIS

I sustain myself
with the love
of family.

MAYA ANGELOU

You don't take a class; you're thrown into motherhood and learn from experience.

JENNIE FINCH

No one puts her family first like my mom, and no one loves and supports me as unconditionally as her.

JENNA DEWAN

I admit it –
you were right
all along!

A MOTHER IS A
PERSON WHO,
SEEING THERE ARE
ONLY **FOUR** PIECES
OF PIE FOR **FIVE**
PEOPLE, PROMPTLY
ANNOUNCES
SHE NEVER DID
CARE FOR PIE.

Tenneva Jordan

A mother knows
what her child's
gone through,
even if she didn't
see it herself.

PRAMOEDYA ANANTA TOER

THE TERM
"WORKING MOTHER"
IS RIDICULOUSLY
REDUNDANT.

DONNA REED

Biology is the least of what makes someone a mother.

Oprah Winfrey

"

THERE IS NO
LOVE AS PURE,
UNCONDITIONAL
AND STRONG AS A
MOTHER'S LOVE.

Hope Edelman

"

THEY SAY
OUR MOTHERS
REALLY KNOW
HOW TO PUSH
OUR BUTTONS
BECAUSE THEY
INSTALLED THEM.

ROBIN WILLIAMS

I am in awe of your wisdom and grace, and I hope I can emulate those ideals with my own child.

JESSICA BIEL
TO HER MOTHER

YOU INSPIRE ME
every day

Mothers possess
a power beyond
that of a king
on his throne.

MABEL HALE

THE MOST
IMPORTANT THING
IN THE WORLD
IS **FAMILY**
AND **LOVE**.

John Wooden

A good mother is irreplaceable.

ADRIANA TRIGIANI

YOUTH FADES,
LOVE DROOPS,
THE LEAVES OF
FRIENDSHIP FALL;
A MOTHER'S SECRET
HOPE OUTLIVES
THEM ALL.

OLIVER WENDELL HOLMES SR

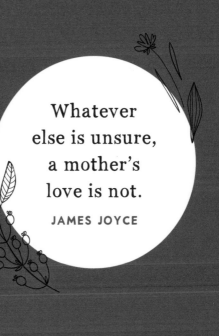

Whatever
else is unsure,
a mother's
love is not.

JAMES JOYCE

I admire her tenacity and her generosity and her ability to do 17 things at once.

MELISSA RIVERS
ON HER MOTHER,
JOAN RIVERS

It may be possible to gild pure gold, but who can make his mother more beautiful?

MAHATMA GANDHI

♥

I HOPE

you know

HOW

special

YOU ARE

♥   ♡   ♥

*The natural state
of motherhood is
unselfishness.*

JESSICA LANGE

In time of test,
family is best.

BURMESE PROVERB

A GOOD MOTHER
LOVES FIERCELY BUT
ULTIMATELY BRINGS
UP HER CHILDREN TO
THRIVE WITHOUT HER.

ERIN KELLY

If at first you don't succeed, try doing it the way your mother told you to in the beginning.

Anonymous

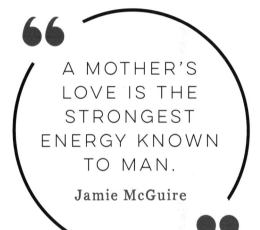

"A MOTHER'S LOVE IS THE STRONGEST ENERGY KNOWN TO MAN."

Jamie McGuire

MOTHERS GIVE
UP SO MUCH,
SO THAT THEIR
CHILDREN CAN
HAVE SO MUCH.

CATHERINE PULSIFER

One of the oldest human needs is having someone to wonder where you are when you don't come home at night.

MARGARET MEAD

You bring out

THE BEST

in me

Mother love is the
fuel that enables a
normal human being
to do the impossible.

MARION C. GARRETTY

MOTHERHOOD:
ALL LOVE **BEGINS**
AND **ENDS** THERE.

Robert Browning

Our mothers
always remain
the strangest,
craziest people
we've ever met.

MARGUERITE DURAS

BEING WHO YOU
TRULY WANT TO
BE — WHO YOU
TRULY ARE — IS
ONE OF THE MOST
IMPORTANT THINGS
MY MOTHER
TAUGHT ME.

KELLY OSBOURNE

My mother
is my root,
my foundation.

MICHAEL JORDAN

It seems to me that my mother was the most splendid woman I ever knew.

CHARLIE CHAPLIN

*Children are
the anchors of
a mother's life.*

SOPHOCLES

You light up
every room

WHO RAN TO **HELP** WHEN I FELL, AND WOULD SOME **PRETTY** STORY TELL, OR **KISS** THE PLACE TO MAKE IT WELL? MY **MOTHER**.

Ann Taylor

Acceptance, tolerance, bravery, compassion. These are the things my mom taught me.

LADY GAGA

SUCCESSFUL MOTHERS
ARE NOT THE
ONES THAT HAVE
NEVER STRUGGLED.
THEY ARE THE
ONES THAT NEVER
GAVE UP, DESPITE
THE STRUGGLES.

SHARON JAYNES

No gift to your mother can ever equal her gift to you – life.

Anonymous

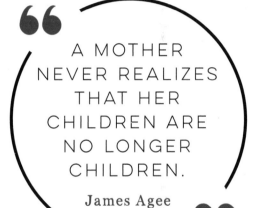

66

A MOTHER
NEVER REALIZES
THAT HER
CHILDREN ARE
NO LONGER
CHILDREN.

James Agee

99

OF ALL THE
RIGHTS OF
WOMEN, THE
GREATEST IS TO
BE A MOTHER.

LIN YUTANG

The mother's heart is the child's schoolroom.

HENRY WARD BEECHER

M♥M IS JUST ANOTHER WORD FOR *home*

For most exhausted mums, their idea of "working out" is a good, energetic lie-down.

KATHY LETTE

MOTHER IS THE
ONE WE **COUNT**
ON FOR THE
THINGS THAT
MATTER **MOST**
OF ALL.

Katherine
Butler Hathaway

There is no velvet so soft as a mother's lap, no rose so lovely as her smile, no path so flowery as that imprinted with her footsteps.

EDWARD THOMSON

MOTHER IS
NOT A TITLE.
MOTHER IS A VERB.
IT IS NOT
WHO YOU ARE.
IT'S WHAT YOU DO.

SHONDA RHIMES

No influence
is as powerful
as that of
the mother.

SARAH JOSEPHA HALE

She's inspiring,
she's strong,
she's funny,
she's creative,
she's talented...
she's everything
that I want to be.

BEYONCÉ ON HER MOTHER

*The patience
of a mother might
be likened to a
tube of toothpaste –
it's never quite
all gone.*

ANONYMOUS

YOU'RE A

M♥m

IN A

million

There is such a special sweetness in being able to participate in creation.

PAMELA S. NADAV

Every beetle is a
gazelle in the eyes
of its mother.

MOORISH PROVERB

MUM ALWAYS SAYS
THE RIGHT THING.
SHE ALWAYS MAKES
EVERYTHING BETTER.

SOPHIE KINSELLA

*My mother's great...
she could stop you
from doing anything,
through a closed
door, even with
a single look.*

Whoopi Goldberg

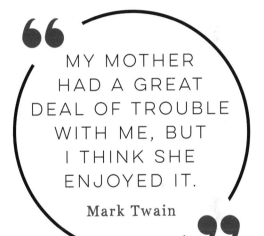

MY MOTHER
HAD A GREAT
DEAL OF TROUBLE
WITH ME, BUT
I THINK SHE
ENJOYED IT.

Mark Twain

A SMART
MOTHER
MAKES OFTEN
A BETTER
DIAGNOSIS
THAN A POOR
DOCTOR.

AUGUST BIER

*Paradise is
at the feet of
the mother.*

ARABIC PROVERB

There are
NO
PROBLEMS
that M♥m
can't fix

To a child's ear
"mother" is magic
in any language.

ARLENE BENEDICT

THINK OF YOUR
MOTHER AND
SMILE FOR ALL
THE GOOD
PRECIOUS
MOMENTS.

Ana Monnar

A mother's kiss
lovingly forgives
the past, present,
and future.

TERRI GUILLEMETS

WHILE WE TRY TO
TEACH OUR CHILDREN
ALL ABOUT LIFE,
OUR CHILDREN
TEACH US WHAT
LIFE IS ALL ABOUT.

ANGELA SCHWINDT

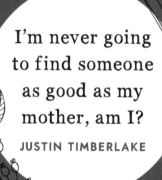

I'm never going to find someone as good as my mother, am I?

JUSTIN TIMBERLAKE

Mothers
always know.

OPRAH WINFREY

There was never a great man who had not a great mother.

OLIVE SCHREINER

Everything I am,
you helped
me to be

YOU WILL **ALWAYS**
BE YOUR CHILD'S
FAVOURITE TOY.

Vicki Lansky

Mother is the heartbeat in the home; and without her, there seems to be no heart throb.

LEROY BROWNLOW

MY MOTHER IS
THE BONES OF MY
SPINE, KEEPING ME
STRAIGHT AND TRUE.
SHE IS MY BLOOD.
SHE IS THE BEATING
OF MY HEART.

KRISTIN HANNAH

A little girl,
asked where her
home was, replied,
"Where mother is."

Keith L. Brooks

A MOTHER UNDERSTANDS WHAT A CHILD DOES NOT SAY.

Jewish proverb

MOTHER -
THAT WAS THE
BANK WHERE
WE DEPOSITED
ALL OUR HURT
AND WORRIES.

THOMAS DE WITT TALMAGE

Parenting is the easiest thing in the world to have an opinion about, but the hardest thing in the world to do.

MATT WALSH

YOU ARE
THE GLUE
THAT BINDS US
all together

To describe my mother would be to write about a hurricane in its perfect power.

MAYA ANGELOU

FAMILY
IS THE MOST
IMPORTANT
THING IN
THE WORLD.

Diana,
Princess of Wales

I am convinced
that this is the
greatest power
in the universe.

N. K. JEMISIN ON MOTHERS

SHE NEVER
QUITE LEAVES HER
CHILDREN AT HOME,
EVEN WHEN SHE
DOESN'T TAKE
THEM ALONG.

MARGARET CULKIN BANNING

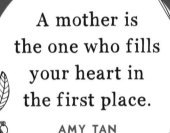

A mother is
the one who fills
your heart in
the first place.

AMY TAN

If love is sweet
as a flower, then
my mother is that
sweet flower of love.

STEVIE WONDER

I thought my mom's whole purpose was to be my mom. That's how she made me feel.

NATASHA GREGSON WAGNER

*No language can
express the power
and beauty and
heroism and majesty
of a mother's love.*

EDWIN HUBBELL CHAPIN

I GET

all

MY BEST
BITS FROM

you!

My mother never
gave up on me.

DENZEL WASHINGTON

THAT'S THE
WONDERFUL THING
ABOUT MOTHERS,
YOU CAN BECAUSE
YOU MUST, AND
YOU JUST DO.

KATE WINSLET

*I realized when you
look at your mother,
you are looking at
the purest love you
will ever know.*

Mitch Albom

66

THERE IS
ONLY ONE
PRETTY CHILD
IN THE WORLD,
AND EVERY
MOTHER HAS IT.

Chinese proverb

99

I LOVE HER
FOR BEING
BRAVE AND FOR
HAVING SUCH
AN IMPORTANT
VOICE IN
MY LIFE.

**SALMA HAYEK
ON HER MOTHER**

Sing out loud
in the car even,
or especially,
if it embarrasses
your children.

MARILYN PENLAND

I know enough to
know that when
you're in a pickle...
call mom.

JENNIFER GARNER

You can fool

SOME
PEOPLE,

but you can't
fool your m♥m

I MAY BE A **NOVICE**, BUT I'M LEARNING FROM THE **BEST**.

Alex Jones
describing her mother
as her role model

Working mothers
are guinea pigs
in a scientific
experiment to
show that sleep
is not necessary
to human life.

ANONYMOUS

I WONDERED IF
MY **SMILE** WAS
AS BIG AS HERS.
MAYBE AS BIG.
BUT NOT AS
BEAUTIFUL.

Benjamin Alire Sáenz
on his mother

*M♥m – you're
the best!*

Have you enjoyed this book?
If so, find us on Facebook at
Summersdale Publishers, on Twitter
at @Summersdale and on Instagram
at @summersdalebooks and get in
touch. We'd love to hear from you!

www.summersdale.com

Image credits

pp.3, 34, 66, 98, 130, 159 © Natalisa/Shutterstock.
com; pp.5, 21, 37, 53, 69, 78, 85, 94, 101, 110, 117, 126,
133, 149 © Maria_Galybina/Shutterstock.com; pp.9,
17, 19, 25, 33, 41, 49, 51, 57, 65, 73, 81, 83, 89, 97, 105,
113, 115, 121, 137, 145, 153 © Julia Henze/Shutterstock.
com; pp.11, 13, 16, 29, 32, 43, 45, 48, 61, 64, 75, 77,
80, 93, 96, 107, 109, 112, 125, 128, 139, 141, 144, 157,
160 © barkarola/Shutterstock.com; pp.15, 31, 47,
63, 79, 95, 111, 127, 143 © avian/Shutterstock.com